Laugh Together

BY TORA STEPHENCHEL

People love to
laugh together.

Parents
laugh together.

Sisters and brothers
laugh together.

Grandparents
laugh together.

Friends
laugh together.

People at work
laugh together.

People at school
laugh together.

Whole families
laugh together.

Even strangers
laugh together.

It is fun to
laugh together!

Sight words are a foundation for reading. It's important for young readers to have sight words memorized at a glance without breaking them down into individual letter sounds. Sight words are often phonetically irregular and can't be sounded out, so readers need to memorize them. Knowing sight words allows readers to focus on more difficult words in the text. The intent of this book is to repeat specific sight words as many times as possible throughout the story. Through repetition of the words, emerging readers will recognize, and ideally memorize, each sight word. Memorizing sight words can help improve readers' literacy skills.

laugh

together

About the Author

Tora Stephenchel lives in
Minnesota. She loves to spend
time with her son, daughter,
husband, and two silly dogs.

The Child's World®
childsworld.com

Published by The Child's World®
1980 Lookout Drive • Mankato, MN 56003-1705
800-599-READ • www.childsworld.com

Photographs © 2xSamara.com/Shutterstock.com: 10; Dean Drobot/Shutterstock.com:
18; Flamingo Images/Shutterstock.com: 13; MidoSemsem/Shutterstock.com: 23; Monkey
Business Images/Shutterstock.com: 17, 21; Olena Yakobchuk/Shutterstock.com: 9;
Phase4Studios/Shutterstock.com: cover, 1, 6; Rido/Shutterstock.com: 5; Robert Kneschke/
Shutterstock.com: 2; wavebreakmedia/Shutterstock.com: 14

ISBN 9781503845121 (Reinforced Library Binding)
ISBN 9781503846562 (Portable Document Format)
ISBN 9781503847750 (Online Multi-user eBook)
LCCN: 2020931112

Printed in the United States of America